MAIN STREET
PUBLIC LIBRARY

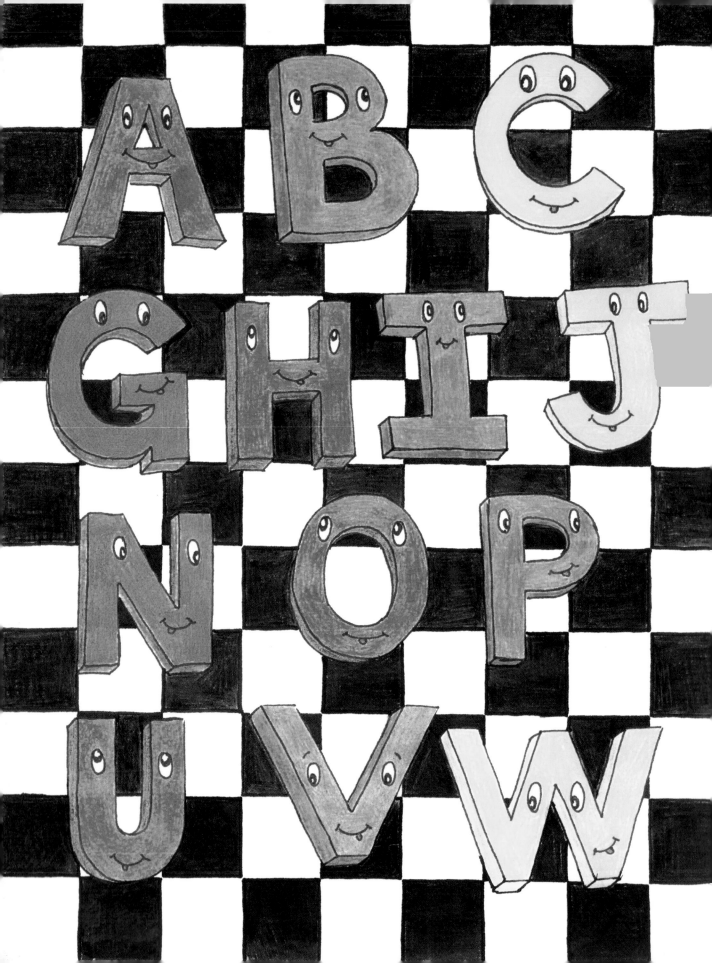

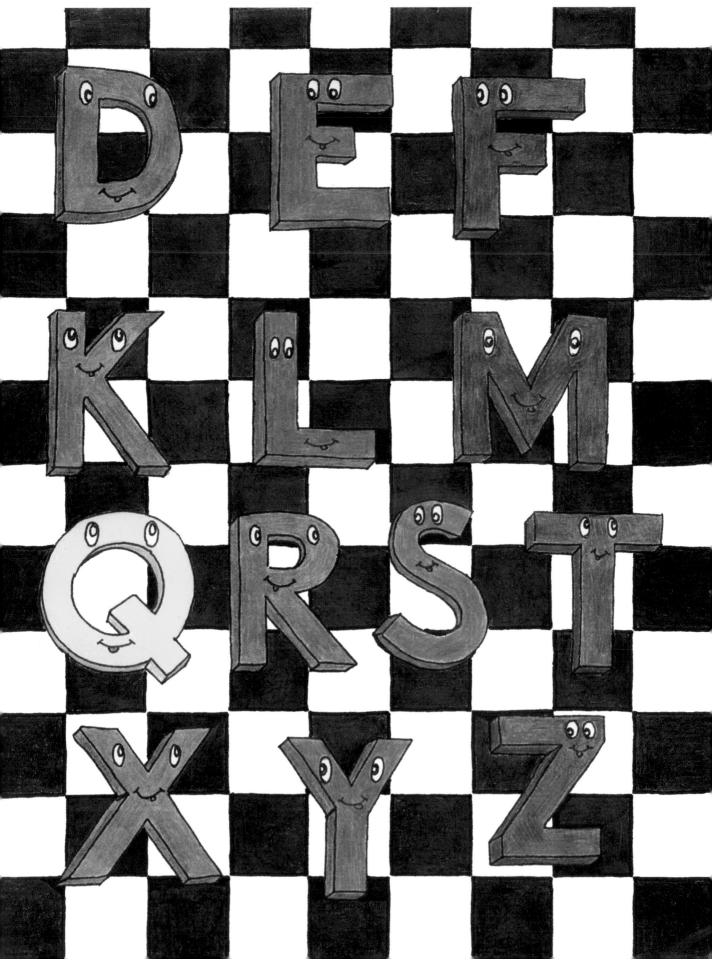

Library books are to share, so we don't write in them. But this book is mine, so we can record some information about me. Then we will remember when I first learned to read.

This **Isn't It Great?** book belongs to:

_____

Date of birth_____

Date of aha! moment_____

Parents: When your child's eyes light up as they understand that letters go together to make words, please register in their book and on our website:

www.birchlakebooks.com

Knowledge is to be shared. To share **Isn't it Great?** with your friends, please order from the website on the where to get **Isn't it Great?** page.

Isn't It Great? © 2010
Sue Oksanen & Riley Zeisler
Illustrations by Tina DeRungs

Birch Lake Books
P.O. Box 62
Barnum, MN 55707

Birch
Lake
Books

www.birchlakebooks.com
birchlakebooks@gmail.com

ISBN-10: 1-4528-7225-2
ISBN-13: 978-1452872254

Library of Congress Control Number: 2010913451

Keywords: Letters/ Words/ Books/ Library/ Community
Category: Juvenile Nonfiction / Readers / Beginner

Printed by Create Space, a member of the Amazon group of companies.

Isn't it Great?

Written by Sue Oksanen
& Riley Zeisler

Illustrated by Tina DeRungs

MAIN STREET
PUBLIC LIBRARY

how letters go together...

Isn't it great how words go together...

The little dog laughed to see such sport. The cow jumped over the moon.

Isn't it great how sentences go together...

Hey diddle, diddle, the cat and the fiddle. The dish ran away with the spoon.

Hey diddle, diddle, the cat and the fiddle.
The cow jumped over the moon.
The little dog laughed to see such sport.
The dish ran away with the spoon

to make a story?

Isn't it great how stories go together...

Isn't it great how a library brings people together...

Hey diddle, diddle. The cat and the fiddle. The cow jumped over the moon. The little dog laughed to see such a sport and the dish ran away with the spoon!

Mary had a little lamb whose fleece was white as snow. And everywhere that Mary went the lamb was sure to go. It followed her to school one day which was against the rule. It made the children laugh and play to see a lamb at school. And so the teacher turned it out but still it lingered near. "What makes the lamb love Mary so?" the eager children cried. "Why Mary loves the lamb you know!" the teacher did reply.

Peter, Peter, pumpkin eater, Had a wife and couldn't keep her. He put her in a pumpkin shell and there he kept her very well.

Little Miss Muffet sat on a tuffet eating her curds and whey. Along came a spider and sat down beside her and frightened Miss Muffet away!

Rub a dub dub, three men in a tub. And who do you think they be? The butcher, the baker, the candlestick maker. Turn them out, knaves all three.

Humpty Dumpty sat on a wall, Humpty Dumpty had a great fall. All the King's horses, and all the King's men, couldn't put Humpty together again!

Jack be nimble! Jack be quick! Jack jump over the candle stick!

Three little kittens they lost their
mittens, and they began to cry,
"Oh mother dear, we sadly fear
that we have lost our mittens."
"What lost your mittens? You naughty
kittens! Then you shall have no pie."
"Meow, meow, meow,
now we shall have no pie."
The three little kittens they found their
mittens, and they began to cry,
"Oh mother dear, see here, see here
for we have found our mittens."
"Put on your mittens, you silly kittens
and you shall have some pie!"
"Meow, meow, meow!
Now let us have some pie."
The three little kittens put on their
mittens and soon ate up the pie,
"Oh mother dear, we greatly fear
that we have soiled our mittens."
"What soiled your mittens?
You naughty kittens!"
Then they began to cry,
"Meow, meow, meow."
Then they began to sigh.
The three little kittens they washed their
mittens and hung them out to dry,
"Oh mother dear, do you not hear
that we have washed our mittens?"
"What washed your mittens? You are good
kittens but I smell a rat close by!"
"Meow, meow, meow
we smell a rat close by!"

Little Boy Blue come blow your horn,
the sheep's in the meadow, the cow's in the corn.
But where's the boy who looks after the sheep?
He's under a haystack fast asleep.

Three blind mice.
See how they run!
They all run after
the farmer's wife.
She cut off their tail
with a carving knife.
Have you ever seen such
a sight in your life as
three blind mice?

Old Mother Hubbard
went to the
cupboard to get her
poor dog a bone.
But when she got
there, the cupboard
was bare and so the
poor dog had none.

Books I Have Read

Isn't it Great? by Sue Oksanen and Riley Zeisler, Illustrated by Tina DeRungs

_____

_____

_____

_____

_____

_____

_____

_____

_____

MAIN STREET
PUBLIC LIBRARY

Books I Have Read

MAIN STREET
PUBLIC LIBRARY

My Favorite Books

My Favorite Words

Order your library card pocket today!

Please send a **$1.00 processing fee** and a **self addressed stamped envelope** to :

Library Card Pocket
Birch Lake Books
PO Box 62
Barnum, MN 55707

Then visit your local library to get your child's first library card.

When your self-adhesive plastic pocket arrives in the mail, center it over "My First Library Card" on the facing page so you can always find your child's library card.

Don't forget to read to your child and with your child every day.

If you would like to receive information of other children's books from Birch Lake Books, include your e-mail address or e-mail us at:

birchlakebooks@gmail.com

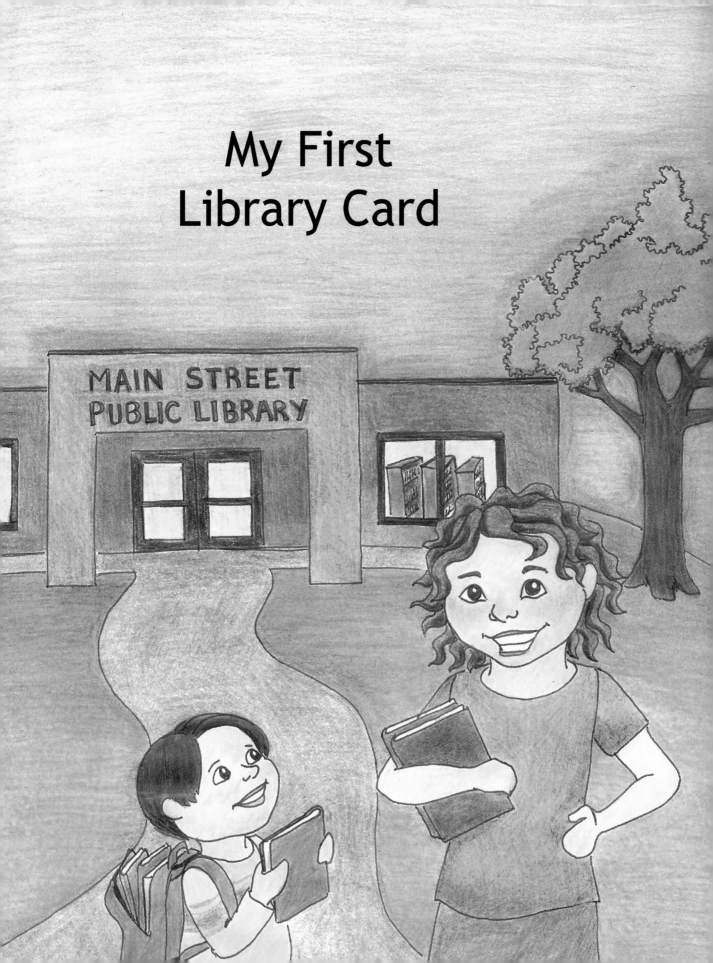

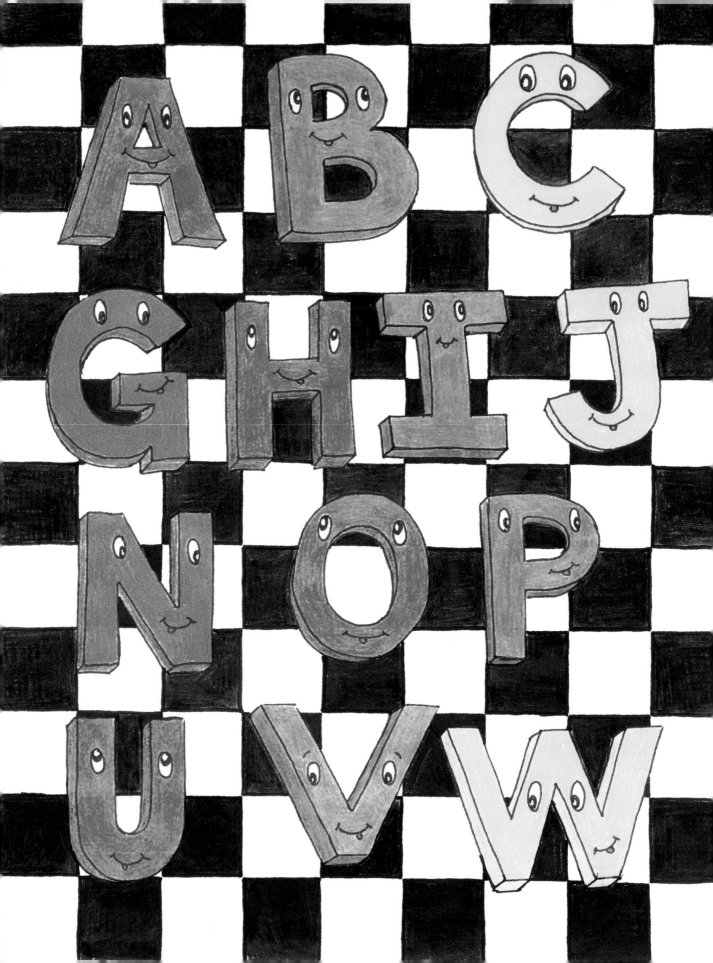

CPSIA information can be obtained
at www.ICGtesting.com
Printed in the USA
LVIC06n1910051213
364042LV00024B/139